NEON SUN

Janette Voski

Neon Sun Copyright © Janette Voski, 2022.

All rights reserved. No part of this book may be reproduced or transmitted in any form or by any means without written permission from the author.

ISBN: 978-0-6485925-6-3

Cover design by Janette Voski. Copyright © 2022.
Interior illustrations by Janette Voski. Copyright © 2022.

Published on 2 February 2022.

Also by Janette Voski

Bones
X

For you, who loves
openly
thoughtfully
passionately
with no reservation
after heartbreak

A paradox:
We all want fierce, final love yet may fear heartbreak.

Only, to remain in fear, courage is not a requirement.
The ability to accept and express love is found in the recognition of trusting that you will overcome pain.

Only when you surrender to the possibility of heartbreak, can you be open to experiencing unfiltered, passionate love in all its glory.

Before You

If I let you into my home

You wouldn't

Steal the furnishings
Leave muddy footprints
Scream ear-splitting.

If I let you into my home

Welcome with a kiss
My home is my heart
Tread gently with bliss.

When I let you into my home

Don't cut off my wings
When you unpack your belongings
Please don't break anything.

Contents

INTRODUCTION ◊ 1

MORNING ◊ 5
00:00
01:00
02:00
03:00
04:00
05:00
06:00
07:00
08:00
09:00
10:00
11:00

AFTERNOON ◊ 19
12:00
13:00
14:00
15:00
16:00

EVENING ◊ 25
17:00
18:00
19:00
20:00

NIGHT ◊ 33
21:00
22:00
23:00

EPILOGUE ◊ 39

INTRODUCTION

The sun already contains neon, but the abundance of neon within the sun is always being questioned by astronomers. It has been stated that neon does not appear in the spectrum of light, visible to the naked eye, but its abundance is shown by how brightly it shines in X-rays. It has been concluded that there is more neon in the sun than originally suspected. To me, the beauty of this is in its inconclusivity. That it simply cannot be measured.

That is what I believe love is. A powerful force that is incendiary. It has the power to spark more than a fire in your heart, because you feel it within your soul. Like fire to touch, the necessary flame that feeds your desire for romance, passion.

Neon Sun is about the kind of love that can consume you but doesn't overwhelm you. Like having the right amount of oxygen to breathe in profusion and enough to keep the fire kindling, without it losing control. The kind of love that whispers its power, because it doesn't need to scream.

Love is powerful and has the intensity to burn you, but never dishonours your hunger for its heat. It is the warmth on my skin and the warmth from within. It is what makes me smile to myself, what makes me bite my lips at its thought and what makes my soul soar. It is just one thing, but many, all at the same time.

We may desire different things, but in the end we all crave the same, don't we? We want to be intimate. We crave to be loved. To see love, feel it, taste it, smell it, and fall asleep in its arms.

We love and have loved so many different people, yet we have never known the same love. To know you can only ever experience that type of love, with that specific person just once in a lifetime … how extraordinary.

Like there are five basic senses, there are five love languages.

NEON SUN

Some say they're one, or the other, but if I had to choose, I feel as though I immerse myself in every single one.

I love you. I know I could just *tell* you I love you, but there is a simmering depth to this feeling that saying it is not enough.

So, in this open love letter, I articulate the way I love you in 24 hours, by the hour.

I have tried to explain a colour that doesn't exist, but it wasn't until I wrote this, I realise *this* is what it is. This is the colour that doesn't exist: Neon Sun.

Neon Sun exists in the way that I view and express love. It exists in the way that love, in all its abundance, can never be measured. It is infinite.

MORNING

Don't rush
Buttons misplaced
Kiss you gently
Every bit of you traced.

00:00

I said I wanted to sleep on love
See if it was better than a pillow

Like thinking it's luck, but knowing it's prayer
I just found out it doesn't compare.

01:00

Like looking with new eyes, I find mystery within you daily
Every second I want to learn more.
If to want is a desire, and to have is to love
Fine line between them, I feel both to their core.

Your eyes match your shirt, earthy tones like seafoam
With iridescence and power of the moon.
Blessings aplenty, your influence inspires intensity
A house in unity is a home, with hearts attuned.

02:00

Fall asleep at one eighty
Your rhythmic breath behind
Soft fingers tickle
As my head weighs heavy on incline.

Wake with your arm tugging my waist
Guiding me with grace
Scooping me too easily toward you
In a tight embrace.

03:00

My soul is on fire, with skin like sunshine, not everybody likes the heat. Passion not mistaken for frustration, with shivers down your spine, you want it concrete. Lava from within erupts, its wave warms, slow yet abrupt, and you take leaps. Always plan your escape with fire safety, no interest in side-burners, charcoal's more tasty. Playing with fire, playing for keeps, you tilt your head as our eyes meet. Prefer the colours of flames to a dulled heart, for me you'd fight. Self-luminous like the sun, even the moon reflects its light. Others try to suffocate the fire while you fully commit, walk with conviction as you prod the firepit. Your grin matures as you reach for my hand, "fire nourishes the soil, many don't understand". Luckily, it's night but I feel my skin turn to scarlet with sensation, as you continue, "allowing for stronger, healthier foundation". Others dash as you guide me on gilded wings, if my heart could speak I know it would sing. Spicy to touch, it tingles. My armour, my alibi. Our toes squeak on the sand, as we land in time to look up at the sky. Light has no darkness, like a shadowless flame. A ring of fire, yes I'll take your name. Fireworks whistle, crack and hiss, my attention fixed as you lean in to kiss. Wind picks up as the fire grows wild, others retreat while you sway back and smile. My desire, my heart, best friend today, tomorrow.
You understand when I can't explain, you whisper:
"pyro".

04:00

He holds it carefully
He cares for it well
He feels it deeply
He's like a citadel.

Points to the shooting star
Grips my arm as it appears
His wish is silent
But I can vividly hear.

His scent is ambrosial
His eyes read aspiration
He caresses my soul
His heart speaks confirmation.

His language, an art
His tongue is his brush
When he speaks in colours
I turn to blush.

Doesn't matter where
Or how long we part
You can't spell it without he
You can't spell it without   art.

05:00

The cloak lifts off, revealing something golden. Sky littered with every colour, all at once. No sunrise and no sunset is ever the same, yet every single time, it is always the most beautiful to watch. It's so fleeting too – a moment passes and the colours drift with the wind. That *blink-and-you-miss-it* kind of thing.

Moments like these remind me why it's important to slow down and be present, to realise what and who you've got.

I turn to look back at you and catch myself in a moment of gratitude. As you slowly move your arms half awake, the colours softly evolve into a golden blanket.

I look to the horizon as the golden crescent continues to rise.
I walk outside and take a deliberate, deep breath.
I feel so light, like I'm breathing in air straight from heaven, and it grants me wings.

Just as the sun wakes up, you do too
Whisper, come watch the clouds shift
Not to disrupt you.

Feel myself dance with all the shades
Greeting me good morning, as I too, drift
Before it all fades.

06:00

Sluggish start to the sunrise
Sleep walking to a seat
Soft manner with your little spitfire
Smooth coffee with a sweet.

You have your father's patience,
With your mother's passion.
I see them fighting within.

Judging by your disarming smile
This time, I'd say you let your father win.

07:00

Part of you feels compelled
Shelter me from wind, rain
But you're intimate with nature
So you watch the hurricane.

Strong roots, look at the canopy
All the fruit, ripe
Worth the wait
Every bit of your hype.

Storm calms with your racing heart
Warning's prescient
Your safety is my home
Boy, you are supremely sentient.

By your side
Magnitude multiplier
Wanted to stop the thunder
Started a fire.

Your altruism is astounding
Know how to ignite
Every temptation, an invitation, and
Boy, do you invite.

08:00

Enough.

Is it enough?
Am I doing enough?
How can I love you more?

We want to create and sustain wholesome, lasting relationships with those we love so much, yet we constantly try to measure if it's enough. But you can't squeeze love into measuring cups, and you can't weigh it.

There is no measure of love, yet you feel expansion.

You may be able to measure expansion of many other things, but you cannot contain something as infinite as love into something as limited as measurement.

What we have is love and with love, comes trust.
Trust that although we cannot see within each other's hearts, we are able to express, to its very depth, what is felt in it.

Enough.

09:00

If the mind learns through repetition
I'll whisper it in your ears
I'll remind you every day
I'll ease all your fears.

If the mind learns through repetition
I'll share my light with you
I'll imitate the sun's rising warmth
I'll sweeten your feverfew.

If the mind learns through repetition
I'll hold your hand when you drive
I'll twirl around you, dancing
I'll make you feel alive.

If the mind learns through repetition
I'll kiss you every chance I get
I'll leave little love notes in your coats
I'll live with no regret.

10:00

Energy's kinetic
Its magnetic pulsating
Looks majestic, stimulating
Electricity reanimating.

Tickle me with trace
Fixity, come face to face
Lost in someplace
Goosebumps in retrace.

Pulsing through your fingers
Charging energy
Mutual unguarded trust
Sensitive to your sensory.

11:00

Passion for art, observing you
Prime architecture, sweetness of honeydew.

If we understood it, it would be plain
Appreciate it, create it, recognise beauty in pain.

Stand-off with a statue, my smile: your command
Camera clicks, as I turn to reach your hand.

Like a tattoo, appears on your skin
Outer appearance changes with every committed sin.

No wonder you're beautiful,
No wonder you're a charm
When you left the museum …

Why didn't they sound the alarm?

AFTERNOON

Golden blanket
Enchanted.

Golden heart
Planted.

12:00

Your unintentional reflection triggers my intentional action.
Let me explain.

If you look overwhelmed,
I'll prepare an orderly list, I'll ask which of them I can do.

If you crave your favourite,
I'll come home with ingredients, I'll cook it for you.

If I recognise a habit,
I'll learn why it started and what it conveys. Like when you tilt your head, I'll know to let you lead us, I'll hold your hand through the maze.

If you reach for a hug in silence,
I'll make you laugh at any cost, no matter how insane.

If you dart your eyes across the room,
I'll find where you left whatever it is, before you even begin to explain.

If you quietly exhale at the traffic,
I'll caress your hair, I'll check the map.

If your gaze becomes thoughtful distress,
I'll rub your back, I'll ask who to slap.

13:00

Quarrels burn out a tealight candle because there's open communication before scandal. Scale no matter how steep, no promises made that we can't keep. Omission is unjust, apologies don't heal broken trust. Surprise with a little gift and love note signed, pure love and affection in mind. Cost is priceless just to see you smile, need me to do something I'll do it in style. Stand still, I'll sneak behind and reach my arms around your waist, to kiss your back until our hands interlace. Share compliments, cute reminders throughout the day, if there were no word limits, I'd submit essays. Every morning with the milk in your coffee, I'll draw a design, and in time,

I'll ask you why it took so long for you to become mine.

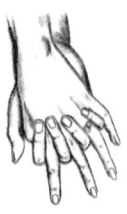

14:00

When I point out a wrinkle
You tell me its story
A story of strength
A story of laughter.

When I point out grey hair
You tell me it's a sign
A sign of good life
A sign that's sought after.

15:00

Rest your head, darling
Four wrinkled lines
An overcrowded forehead
One day each until Valentine's.

You're safe here
All love, no landmines
Capacity overflowing, more to give
Moulded over time.

I'll softly stroke your skin
I'll share your silence.

16:00

Running through fields of our garden, as if it were a maze
Yelling you'll always find me
Yelling you'll catch me in every way.

Crystal water glistening, inviting, reaching through the sun's rays. Diving right in, I know, you know, not just the sun ablaze. You're catching up, laughter a craze. Jumped right out, slipping from your grasp, we don't even know the day. Running back through the flowers, as if it were a race, as if we were opposing, suppose I'll relax my pace … Chuckle in my defiance, ready for your arms to wrap me, trying to catch our breath, finally you catch me.

Lost near a fountain, as if it were a maze
Whispering you'll always find me
Whispering you'll catch me in every way.

EVENING

Heart a muscle
Mind a weapon
Body of wires
Soul on fire.

Moon full
Stars luminate
Sky's brown
Sundown.

17:00

Gentle jazz gradually gets louder as I make my way downstairs. At first, not quite loud enough to conceal my echoing footsteps. Candles lit, two empty wine glasses, and a bowl of freshly-washed blackberries and cherries. I walk closer to find a cream envelope resting against a long, lone candle addressed to:

My Love.

The envelope is way too well positioned to have not been a deliberate *open me when you see this*. I reach for it and tear the back open like I used to unwrap Christmas gifts as a kid. Carefully, not to rip it, but with such urgency that it still does.

I look behind me to wonder where you are as I gently unfold the letter with paper that feels like silk.

I already picture your face riddled with perplexity as you read. Maybe you're also wondering where I've gone.

I went to get something for an exceptional woman with even better taste. I also just had to fill the car with petrol ... but, full disclosure, I needed an excuse to remind you that I see you. Every day, I see your struggles, I see your strength, and I see the way you love. Me and everyone else in your life. The way I know you're strong, but still feel the need to protect you. The way your passion, love, and compassion speak languages unbeknownst to literature. I have never met anyone quite like you, know that I never will, and that is its own blessing. It is an honour to call you mine.

Your stubbornness may irritate me, but your eyes! The way your doe eyes speak when you look up at me, no matter if your lips remain still. Like being static in the middle of a forest, for that is when nature becomes loud. Your compelling smile, the way it can change the weather. Both, my greatest distractions ... ah, but welcome ones. I picture you rolled your eyes at the first part, but are you smiling now?

I do, and I am.
I exhale in a chuff as I keep reading.

I love you.

I know I could have just written "I love you", but I wanted to do something different. Something you'll never forget, because you have shown me a love I never will. You crave the perfect amount of adventure and calm — so much so, it's given me new definition to the words 'brave' and 'peace'. Yours is after all, the only presence I crave to be in apart from my own.

I'll be home soon, and when I return, I know you'll look up at me with those same, beautiful eyes I feel both weakened and strengthened by.

For when you find a woman with a heart of gold, you don't try to bend it, and you don't break it.

You make sure it melts.

18:00

I know I'm not the tallest, but you sure are looking down.

For skin like silk, you look like sandpaper.
Did you forget who you are?
We aren't doing that any more, I thought we agreed.
Get dressed by quarter past, get ready to leave.

You forget it doesn't need to be easy, it needs to be worth it.
And worth it … is you.
Don't outrun your sense of orientation when it's time to jog
your memory, don't bite more than you can chew.
I'll recite your own advice, and if you need it, repeat it twice.
Hand me your worries, and your worries will split.
"Are you ready? Great, get in the car, use my scarf as a
blindfold, and sit.
Wait, what are you doing?" I ask, as you run ahead.
You still open my door and kiss my forehead.

I won't answer where we're going or why, you'll just find out.
Nothing like spontaneity and no doubt.

I shift the gears as your hands grip the door in silence.
Once in a while we all need some guidance.
The jolts between gears represents adversity.
There's nothing in life that involves no artistry.
With safety, the car reaches a halt.
Your hands reach to the blindfold in default.

As I help untie the scarf, I say:
"If I stayed in the middle of this parkway,
You wouldn't know it because you couldn't see.
Before I move … answer.
Do you trust me?"

"It's a little late for that," you laugh, as your hand grips my
thigh. Dropping the handbrake with a giggle, I think I caught
you by surprise.

NEON SUN

Count how many things you could see and recall what went through your mind, including the part when I stopped and almost got fined. When you're blinded, your mind assumes much worse, it plays tricks.
You just need to open your eyes to have that fixed.

Now tell me how many times you find your reflection, let's play a little game. Whenever you do,
I want you to really *see* yourself,
I want you to say your name.

The problem is, you're used to your qualities, you don't see what others see, and if you could see yourself through my eyes, you'd see you're exemplary.
You look unsure so I'm setting things straight, you invested in yourself, none of your assets depreciate.

"Tell me honestly, what do you see?"
"I see what you see," a smile forms on his flawless face,
"I see a woman who will not give up on me."

Big eyes look hopeful
Now I'm drowning in brown
Your skin gets brighter
As the sun goes down.

Spray your scent of success that encircles you
Share it around
But don't waste one drop, and
Darling, don't you ever drop your crown.

19:00

Champagne and canapes catered, gowns and suits dressed to perfection. Shaking hands with shaky speech, find comfort as your eyes find my direction.

Bubbly isn't my taste, but it's my temperament, so I sip and smile from a distance. Our eyes flirt across the filled room, but only one in existence.

Raise a toast, I want to thank the ones who raised you. Remember when we met? Best thing I ever bumped into.

Your scent is enough to get me tipsy, but I'm only two sips in. My fingers trace my collarbone, reminds me of your soft skin.

How can I miss you when you're ten metres away? You gesture something foreign, as a single drink appears on a silver tray.

"I hear you're the type to prefer charming combinations," smiles the attendant. We both laugh, as I respond, "How much did he tip you to say that?"

Gentle hands reach my back, accompanied by a soft breeze of wind. I could never mistake that scent, my lips reach for your cheek as you grin.

Raising the glass to my lips, I taste a real drink, I taste reality The one I'm holding and the one who's holding me.

Your eyes on me you kept, you're a keeper.
You are the type I'd regret not keeping years later.

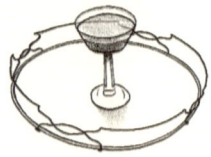

20:00

I'll take the *I love you*'s literally,
Because that's how it's meant when it's said.

It's not love if it's expressed on a whim. It's not love if it dangles above your head like a reward. Love isn't conditional or transactional.

Love doesn't boast of the future, love is patient in the now. Like an eternal flame, emitting through every pulse: a warm wave with every heartbeat. It gives some a sense of direction, in the way the sun, the moon and stars help with navigation.

Love is irrefutable and exults in loyalty and truth. Like the sun, love radiates intensity to your innermost, otherwise unpredictable and contagious emotions.

That's why your heartbreak feels twice as painful. That's why you hesitate before committing yourself to another. Learn to trust everyone: to trust they will be themselves, just as you are. Your definition of and ability to express love may differ from others, and it's important to understand that. But in the end, we can't bid the sun, the moon and stars to budge, just as we can't bid ourselves to begin, or cease loving someone. Love is grander than we are. You may seek it and submit to it, but in no way can you command it. You can't even prevent someone from loving you. Love is a glorious emotion and action that can't be contained, caged between bars, and it most definitely knows no law.

So, I'll continue to take the *I love you*'s literally,
Because that's how it's meant, when it's said.

NIGHT

You make our home a heaven
How high can I get?

Candlelight exposing our kisses in silhouette.

21:00

Pocket full of sunshine
Palm full of the moon
Undivided attention
Fingertips reaching to no tune

Life with new breath
Goosebumps in the cold
Wrap you in my arms
Feel yours unfold.

22:00

Comfortable like the warmth of liquor
Gets stronger every time.

Chemistry and compatible
You want me by your side.

Carry my legs to your lap
Moon provides the light I feel.

Rest my head on your broad shoulders
Solace seeming surreal.

Smooth like a swirl of scotch
Steady in your hands.

Reach to take a sip
Seems you have better plans.

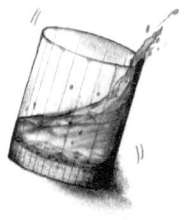

23:00

Your life is your universe, and you are the designer of your very own solar system. No matter how many planets, no matter how many stars, they're all different. Their appearance contrasts, their temperature fluctuates, they spin at special speeds. Gravitational interactions and energy omissions can make an impact on which way the planets and stars get pulled, but none of them spin around you, none of them live for you. Just know, at one moment in time, they needed you to exist. No matter how far they travel from you, no matter how infrequently you meet, each need to continue to follow their own law. Even if it's the last time you ever get to witness their magnetism, be in their orbit … you know not all stars are clusters, not all are bound together by their mutual attraction.

Here, where the presence of gravity allows your feet to rest faultlessly on sound foundation, lies a simple question.

Do you want to remain on solid ground?
Or would you rather

F l o a t ?

EPILOGUE

In many ways, the sun reminds me of love. The way it produces its own energy ... light ... heat. The way the sun is consistent – it always shines, always remains bright: through the clouds, ready for the storm, and even when it's time for the moon to share its light. It's within this consistency that love is found. Regardless of the swaying weather, it remains still, and radiates its rays until the clouds deter, the storm subsides, the moon rests. It is then that you feel it but understand: it has always been there.

I love you in the way that I hope you always feel the sun. That your thirst is quenched by a drop of water, and your hunger satiates by a bite. That your laughter continues to echo ... echo. That your pain leaves your body when my lips meet it. That your eyes be filled with light, and you continue to see beauty: your own, and in the world. That strangers turn into, and remain, friends. That you remember who you are. And if you do forget, I hope you know I will remain like the sun. Because if we established that love cannot be measured by our acts or many languages, we can depict it through the most important language. In the silent expression from the heart, spirit and soul.

So from this point forward I will declare:
I love you like the Neon Sun.

Foundation before structure
Soul over flesh.

@janettevoski

www.ingramcontent.com/pod-product-compliance
Lightning Source LLC
Chambersburg PA
CBHW020331010526
44107CB00054B/2068